welcome yourself home.

you are the destination.

-ZKD-

MARTIAN

-POETRY & PROSE-

BY: ZACHRY K. DOUGLAS

CH.1

~EARTH~

the nights remind me of the love i've
never had, but even in the darkness,
the moon has never left me.

she has shown me how to be at
peace with the light inside of me.

we talk in a way that accounts for the
days where silence was the only thing
we had to hold onto.

you speak in colors and fragrances
which remind me of my younger
years. back when i could love
anything for simply understanding
who i was and what i couldn't say.

love me or leave me. i am tired of guessing who you will be in the morning. i am tired of keeping my heart from the war. i am tired of assuming you will be someone else who doesn't know what they want.

close your eyes and point to your chest.

show me that you can lead yourself to

love. show me your purpose. show me

how to live with intent on being strong

when you feel every broken part of

your life.

~i'm not from here~

i know this fore sure. my bones are
fragmented stars. my eyes are black
holes. my soul is a million years old.
my heart was forged by galaxies
colliding. i am no average human.
i don't even know if i am, human.

you took my hand and showed me

where you go when the night comes.

you showed me how the dawn moves.

you showed me how flesh can be a

flower and house the most important

and fragile parts of life.

my dreams are no longer keeping

me awake. i sleep with your contours

placed around me, as if you were

mother earth herself; sheltering me

from my demons.

i howl at the moon like a madman, like an aged rolling stone. i scream at the sight of stillness. i bleed from the fingers when my grip can no longer take hold. there is so much to this place that takes, and even then, it will never rid all of me from living on in the next world.

the way you rise and
touch the sky above
us, gives reason to
how the universe
creates certain souls
to be loved for simply
looking at you when
no one else ever
could.

i saw you the other day. you were by
yourself for the first time since you left
him. i wandered towards you but
knew if i got too close you would
never live to your potential. it wasn't
that i didn't want you to be mine.
i just knew time has a way of
beginning and stopping when the
energy is right. my god, you looked
so beautiful. too much to be in my
world. maybe one day i can have
your magic co-exist with the man i
wish to be. maybe then our hearts
will be able to speak while we sit
with each other, wrapped up like
the stars in the sea.

you never had to say a goddamn thing.
i knew you were hurting. i knew he was
losing who he was. i knew then how a
human could suffer, yet still love someone
they needed to leave. our lives are based
on the rules we break for those we think
can love us the same.

we oftentimes give our love to those who don't understand it. somehow, we force happiness where it doesn't belong. where it has no fucking business being. we create our heartache long before the stability is settled, and then we act as if it wasn't supposed to break.

the rain falls and i look over at the pecan
trees from the chair where my grandfather
used to to eat, talk to us about politics, his
childhood, the music industry, and the
struggles he went through as a young
man. i can still hear his voice behind me,
as if there was no such thing as death.
i look out the window once again, and
there is the man who died, but lived his
best life teaching us kids how to survive
on peanut butter crackers and buttermilk.
even though he is gone, his steps are still
being counted by so many he left behind.

to the wild existing within the beauty of your bones:

       always choose love.

it hurts because it wasn't supposed to be a lesson. not everything needs a beginning to know how real and meaningful it all was.

come to me, sweet woman.

love me for the mistakes
i am. i will wait until the
space between us
becomes a tomb,
buried by the time
wasted never giving
into what had been
there since we found
a reason to learn the
name of the other.

we are all looking for something.
sometimes we go years without
ever discovering what it is. if you
find yourself amongst the darkness,
just know it will use you as a guiding
light when you are ready.

my father sits in the rocking chair
by the sliding glass door. he speaks
to his mother with adoration and
comfort. this kitchen has shown me
how to love and be around family
even when i didn't feel like i fit in.
it has shown me patience and
resolve by overcoming the hate
living outside of these walls.
a hate that poisons the lives
of so many youthful humans.
this will be remembered long
after our home no longer
includes our souls.

    ~the bricks will eventually be
    torn down, but our love will
    continue building for others~

CH.2

~JUPITER~

speak to me, tell me how i can help.
all i want is for you to not worry about
what you cannot control. i'll tell you
the truth when there is only that to say.
my life begins and ends with you, sweet
soul. everything before you, was only
there to help me get to you. my sunsets
are a dying wish without a love like yours.

be still, my love, your stars are showing again. be still, my love, the universe is ours to play in as long as we keep the love alive and in sight of everything else we are trying to build together.

the body will die, but love
remains above the ground.

nothing feels better than finally
being where you're supposed
to be and being who you were
meant to be.

i've missed you since the day the world organized its thoughts. i can only hope the chaos i am in will bring me back to you. between your heart and stars is where life greets you. we are the moments we fight for to have a beautiful life.

the only time i saw her was under a full

moon. i've never been the same since.

even my darkness fell in love with the

way she conducted the night.

i'm here for as long as it takes for my star to die. for my purpose to grow and bloom. for my eyes to kiss every dream they are opened to. i'm here for love, and maybe the devil is the creator of most of our pain, but i will put my hands around his throat if he ever thinks of touching you.

we walked in the snow, travelers from the
south, begging for redemption with glass
on our tongues. our feet began to sink as
we continued searching for hope. snow
up to our hips, we marched on like soldiers,
looking for the flag. when the sun melted
our only problem, the water kept us alive.

i see you through the forest,
under a blanket of leaves.
you never said a word, but
you kept me company.
the wilderness brings out
the wolves feeding on our
pride, but if that means
being with you now, they
will never take us alive.

the stars match your bones, constructed from the constellations themselves. you speak to me in truths, with mother nature being your center. the jupiter in you breathes for love, and only love.

i wonder if the universe knew what you'd
become if you ever believed in yourself?
i can only hope that it would be proud of
the human doing supernatural things to
save the life you've created.

i could tell he changed you from the woman i once knew. you had fallen away from life, like a burning arrow through the night. somehow you managed to go on well beyond the imagination of the cosmos, dancing in the twilight. your light still speaks to me when i close my eyes. i know you are happy now. i know you've won the battle at the gates of your last stand. live on, wild woman, live on.

even if your heart breaks, love more.
there isn't anything worse in life than
believing you are your own pain.

it doesn't get to dictate your power,
nor does it get the final say.

all dogs are part human.
sometimes they feel more
emotions than we do and
at all times they give more
love than we can.

in every part of your life,

love is the entire flower,

blood and all.

we talk about the same
stories in our lives to bring
out an occurrence of when
happiness overcame the
sadness of moving on to
the next part of our story.
a part that although
created space, it never
got lost in time. we tell
these same stories to
remember that we can
find it again and again,
when all else feels lost.

we must not lose our sense of human connection. if we lose that, we miss out on the moments to express how much we actually hurt when someone asks us how we feel.

look beyond the fire and you will see that
you've always been the untamed chaos
staring back. you've always been a heart
made from moon rocks and hidden valleys.
one that is whole without needing
someone else to be free.

i once wrote a love letter to myself and asked for forgiveness. i asked to be loved again. i asked for closure so i could move on with my life. i asked to be forgotten, because no one should have to remember hell being a human.

today, i mailed it off.

today, i found love again.

the remaining trees spoke of ancient times.
back when they were loved for their shade
and colors. back when they gave us a
reason to pay attention to nature instead
of destroying it.

love demands to be magic between

a coronation of souls once torn apart

by a cosmos still trying to understand

its power. love is ready when you are.

CH.3

~SATURN~

be honest with your intentions. do not go into love knowing you are not on the same page and then begin skipping chapters to finish a book you never wanted to read and keep.

humans will always need their space.
whether it is another room, a different
vehicle, or the moon. some days call
for more distant travels.

~may your wings never taste defeat~

out of her eyes grew tiny universes. all designed by the love she had created inside. all falling slowly enough to know how strong you have to be to cry. all were for the moments she felt weakened by someone who never saw the roses behind her heart. everyone has a breaking point. everyone gets there, but nobody should feel alone at any time. life tends to get simpler once you begin listening to your own pain.

stars we are and monuments we shall become. our defining moment is ahead. our wildness rages on. take a chance on yourself. you are ready for a life-changing experience.

she sits alone with her thoughts
while the world around her keeps
spinning, hoping she discovers a
way to love again. a world like
this one needs a love like hers to
endure the agony living
underneath its skin.

there is nothing like being comforted by the
fact that no one else will ever be who you
are. once you realize that, you will stop
wasting your time handing out pieces
of your soul at a discounted price.

she looked like jazz, all made up
and without needing a reason to
be beautiful. she just was, and
to hear her speak, you knew her
heart was made from the finest
rhythms and colors, all the while
breathing in the fire.

if you want to be happy, let go of the idea that everyone will stay and no one will hurt you. find happiness to be a flower in the weeds and be thankful for the sunshine when you get it. maybe one day you'll understand even weeds can be beautiful, too. life is better understood when speaking to nature.

you love too much, and that's okay.
some people are born to give
everything for brief second, if it means
being a part of something else besides
their own pain.

~even angels can lose
their way in the flames~

all of the galaxies love you.

you've always been stardust

and super moons calling

earth home.

between the night sky and saturn, i see where i was made. between the lightning strikes and thunderous emotion, my name was raised. i speak in rain formed from the mountain springs. i am a minor planet, too close to be a soul, too far away to be a human.

they told me jesus would save me.
that everything you did he saw.
they told me to act right and never
cuss or drink or smoke. they told me
hell was for sinners and heaven only
allowed the pure. they told me to
memorize their lines and forgive others
who hurt you. they told me love founded
their church and all the members gave
back. they told me anything to get me
to stay. i wandered too far off the ledge
of humanity, but i found the same thing
without the judgment and resentment,
without the lies and hypocrites on a side
of a mountain. i found my love, religion,
own service to be amongst. up there,
all you have to do is walk with giants
who accept you as you are.

we swing into the stars without a care to drag us down. our earth becomes our soul. our universe becomes our purpose. there will always be a yesterday, but not another time to be free.

kids teach us about the joys of life.

within a single laugh from them,

your worries float away and for

a brief moment become the

child who had to grow up too

fast in order to help those

around you.

i walked on the moon today. leaving my worries to be planted in the vastness in front of me. i lifted the stars. there is a place for everyone, even if you are alone, you will find your center.

maybe i'm meant to be alone forever.
maybe some people are more whole
than needing anyone else. i've never
understood those who find reasons to
throw their hands up when you should
keep them in the earth around you.

most days i hate myself. then you show me
how to love. you taught me how to finally
carry myself freely with good intentions
and confidence. my backbone remains
upright because of your willingness to
sacrifice for the greater good of who
we are.

bring kindness to me. i'm too old in

existence for anything but a self-less

type of vibration and relationship.

we want love, mostly not to be alone,
but to never feel left out of something
that could be real.

more than dust, we rise with the fading of night. wander amongst the lost and you will find your way. the doubt is only there to make you appreciate the journey.

CH.4

~MERCURY~

all there is for us,
is everything we
are willing to lose
just to touch the
wild embers we
create.

live on. breathe in.
choose the chaos.

stand for the love
fighting inside of
you.

life is about knowing
who and what to
give your energy to.

take a sip of the milky way and tell me
you do not feel something magical.
nothing will last forever, but sometimes
it doesn't have to in order for us to know
that love comes back eventually in the
form of a new day.

flowers made her forget the pain.
she began putting them in her hair
at an early age to keep others from
touching what was gone, what had
been taken away. what she thought
made her beautiful. she is her own
garden now. someone who speaks
kindness to the living and teaches
them you are not what you lose in life.

every so often we come across the moon
during the birth of the sun. walk into the
dawn and breathe in the lost stars of
your home.

let go of the madness, but never surrender to the struggle. life will take you where you need to grow. open yourself up to new sensations, new feelings, new possibilities, new love, new skin.

where there is the

faintest of light,

begin there and

watch the sky

grow for you.

here beneath my feet, gives me reason enough to find more adventures, more life, and more love. being alive takes grit. even more so when the fire couldn't set me free.

take with you the pieces they left and learn that you are not meant to be loved in fractions. you are defined by the light that gets in and shares its secrets of how to survive in the dark. we are given this life to wildly explore. anything less and you are missing out on your full potential.

there is immense magic in the soul
who has tasted death, only to have
made a better environment for its
body to thrive in.

nothing is ever as bad as it seems. it's just as bad as we have it in our minds. we must begin there and unroll and organize the negative thoughts.

i'm not sure if we are ever going to be more than we are now. i just hope it's enough for you yo at least want to try and make it special.

my lost feels better than being found.
leave me with the stars when you feel
like you're getting close.

tears are reminders why it hurt, but they also show us how to start over again. maybe life is just reliving your past until you learn how to move on with it all and become your own reason for letting go.

understanding why you're here has nothing to do with who is in or out of your life. it has everything to do with how you approach yourself when life won't let go of who you used to be.

i just want it to be you when it matters.

    the only place i will ever know love, is when your eyes are looking at me.

with each new breath, our hearts find their
fight. never forget that love is always on the
line. learn from what happened at a
distance. never go back to the cause.
after all, a broken heart can still be loved.

on days where you are full of the sun,
there is always more room for the light.
there is always a chance to learn from
what the darkness doesn't show us.
open yourself up to what it truly is;
a teacher we didn't know we needed.

she had already lived a thousand years. i just wanted to be worth what she had already been through.

when i think about the life i want, it's always been me, her, and the universe under the same stars.

CH.5

~MARS~

we are all martians to the feelings we
oftentimes hide behind. let the moon
in. whatever you do, let her in.

there is green skin underneath this flesh.
distant planets circling inside of my chest.
dust from a lifetime ago made by the
chaos i initiated. dark matter covers my
younger years. i took a walk today to
figure out if it needs to be talked about.
to see if other life forms feel as i do. to see
if this reality truly makes sense to the angels
and devils before me.

i kissed her, and i knew after being that close to someone again, i would never repeat the process of sabotaging my happiness because of my insecurities. her body taught me how lives are connected before we are born.

how the strings of atoms align with the cosmos breathing in us. the strings that pull me ever so close to being who i never gave a chance to in the beginning.

i often wander off too far for some,
but distance away from everything
has never caused me to rethink
anything.

        the further away,
        the closer i am to
        my truth.

at the end of every day, i give thanks
to those who left me in my own misery.
i've never allowed their absence to
impact my decision to love even harder
than before. i love, love, too much to be
changed by those who never leave the
comfort of their own shadow.

no one will ever be able to tell you how much the heart can hold or come back from. i just hope yours can withstand the days you do not feel worthy of what's inside.

not everything will last a lifetime,
but maybe, just maybe,

a moment is all it takes to make
you brave enough to love again.

we are all in search of something that can help us feel worthy of making the next day mean more than the hell we've already been through.

life is the love you are willing to give.

give yourself a chance by learning to

love who you are.

i've never wanted to be the reason why others hurt. i've never been afraid of being misunderstood. i tried to kill who i was to forget about the pain i was in .

i would have missed out on the greatest days of my life, because i had forgotten how to live for a few hours.

some days it takes me a little longer than
most to remember who it is looking back
at me in the mirror. on those days, i can
only hope you see someone who is finally
okay to try again.

earth is still so foreign to me. the smells.
the sites. the people. the sounds, it feels
like i am breathing for the first time each
morning i wake up alone. it gives me
hope that tomorrow the empty side
of the bed next to me will be holding
someone else who once the same way.

within these bones, i've carried graves that never belonged to me. they've taught me how you can still survive the pain and find love in whatever memory is attached to it.

love is the maker of the soul.
it only asks us to remember
how it feels to be left and
never give that to anyone
we come into contact with.
never lend out what you
keep in. allow it room to
grow until you are ready
to understand its power.

death kisses us all. we can only hope that when it does, it allows us to keep living in another way with what we have learned while visiting this place.

be wherever that makes makes your heart bloom. especially during the moments of torrential flooding of soil and sky.

breathe in the wilderness to find your spirit.
only in nature do our true thoughts have a
voice.

it is in the pain you will find who you really
are. who was meant to be a warrior and
one who lays down their armor in defeat.
if you are too be anything, be someone
who fucking fights to live on despite
the wounds you carry.

there are pieces of me everywhere,
yet i have never been more whole.
life has never made as much sense
to me now that i am comfortable
with the feelings inside of me.

now i know where they need to
be directed and how to attain
the moments i am aspiring to
obtain and make.

www.ingramcontent.com/pod-product-compliance
Lightning Source LLC
Chambersburg PA
CBHW021957290426
44108CB00012B/1106